A. C Arvisenet

Communion prayers for every day of the week

A. C Arvisenet

Communion prayers for every day of the week

ISBN/EAN: 9783741163791

Manufactured in Europe, USA, Canada, Australia, Japa

Cover: Foto ©Andreas Hilbeck / pixelio.de

Manufactured and distributed by brebook publishing software (www.brebook.com)

A. C Arvisenet

Communion prayers for every day of the week

COMMUNION PRAYER

FOR

Every Day of the Week

BY

CANON A. C. ARVISENET.

London:
THOMAS RICHARDSON AND SON
AND DERBY.

Preface.

Père Eymard, founder of the Order of Priests of the Most Holy Sacrament, says our Lord in Holy Communion is like a treasure in a casquet, which remains useless till the casquet is broken open, and that it is a good thanksgiving which opens the casquet, and causes the treasure of virtues and graces to flow over into the soul and transform it. One great help towards a good preparation and thanksgiving is a variety of devotional prayers. The following forms may be used on the day of the week to which they are assigned, or such a selection may be chosen as gives the most relish.

The rule for frequent Communion is the profit reaped by it. In the parable of the sower, our Lord says that the good ground brought forth, some thirty, some sixty, and some a hundred-fold. Our Lord is given as the seed in Holy Communion; but perhaps we are discouraged because with such good seed we do not bring forth a hundred-fold. Perhaps we do not even bring forth sixty-fold. We should not, however, withdraw from frequent Communion on this plea, for if we bring forth only thirty-fold, our Lord will still praise us as good ground:—if we can honestly say that our Communions do us good, keep us from evils, and make us more fruitful in virtue; we may then rest satisfied that we have at least the thirty-fold. When the ground is not very rich, a gardener sets his plants closer to each other, that by their multitude he may get some compensation for their want of spread; so imperfect souls stand sometimes more in need of frequent Communion than the perfect.

The prayers are translated and adapted from "The Memorial of a Priestly Life."

Communion Prayers.

SUNDAY.—BEFORE COMMUNION.

1. INTENTION.—O God, most high and most powerful, to the praise and glory of Thy sovereign majesty, as a memorial of the most holy life, passion, and death of Jesus Christ my Saviour, in thanksgiving for all Thy gifts and benefits bestowed on me, an unworthy sinner, and on Thy whole Church, in atonement for all my numberless sins, for my own salvation, and that of N. N., for the relief of the departed N. N., etc., I, a miserable sinner, desire to receive with worship the mysteries of the Body and Blood of Thy Son. Verily, O Lord, in Thee alone is all that can satisfy the desire of my heart. For what have I in heaven but Thee, and what beside Thee do I desire upon earth? Art not Thou Thyself our reward exceeding great?

2. CONTRITION.—But I would offer Thee, O my Lord, together with the Sacrifice and Sacrament of the Body and Blood of Thy Son, the sacrifice also of a troubled spirit. I grieve from my inmost heart that I have ever offended Thee by my sins, especially by N. N., which Thou knowest already, Thou searcher of hearts, who hast been so kind to me, and hast so often fed me

in this Sacrament. I confess them, wretched sinner that I am, sorrowing over them in the bitterness of my soul. Would that I had never offended Thee. But a contrite and humble heart Thou wilt not despise, Thou who hast given us Thine Only-begotten to wash us from our sins in His Blood.

3. Faith.—I firmly believe, O good Jesus, and with a lively faith confess that Thou, very God and Man, equal to the Father in power and glory, art truly and really present in this Sacrament, for Thou the very Truth hast said, "This is My Body." I believe whatsoever the Son of God has said. Nothing is truer than this word of truth. O Lord, help my unbelief, increase my faith.

4. Hope.—O my Lord Jesus Christ, I am only dust, ashes, and a sinner, but Thou art the Father of mercies, and God of all consolation. Who has ever understood all the fulness of Thy mercies? Those, that travail and are heavy laden, dost not Thou call to Thyself, that Thou mayest give them rest? Art not Thou my strong refuge? To whom else should I go? Thou alone hast the words of eternal life, Thou alone dost give comfort in all my tribulation. I am sick and feeble : Thou art my health. Those that are well need not a physician, but those that are sick. If, then, in passing by Thou dost heal all, if the shadow of Peter healed the sick, ought not I to trust that when Thou comest into my house, and dwellest

in me with the fulness of Thy Godhead, I shall also be healed from all my infirmities.

Though, then, I am not conscious to myself of anything, yet will I arise and go to my Father, my Physician, my strong Refuge, hoping that this Communion may bring me an increase of faith, hope, and charity; may guard me safe against the snares of all my enemies; may chase away shameful thoughts; may root out from me the vice and defect of N.; may plant in me every work that is pleasing to Thee, and especially the virtue of N.; and may, in fine, be to me a pledge of glory everlasting. This hope is laid up in my bosom, for Thou art kind and merciful, and Thy promises stand most sure.

5. CHARITY.—O most sweet Saviour Jesus Christ, how great was the vehemence of that love which drew Thee out of the bosom of the Father to take upon Thee our human nature in this vale of tears, and to undergo so many miseries and injuries, even to the death of the cross, and this for us miserable sinners and for our salvation.

Oh, what love! Thou mightest justly have condemned us to hell, but didst rather will to save us. We were guilty, and Thou the innocent didst bear the penalty, that we the guilty might be set free.

It was from love that Thou didst take flesh for us, and so, when leaving the world to return to Thy Father, Thou didst leave Thy Flesh in Sacrament to us as a pledge of love, so that in a new and most wonderful way Thou mightest remain with us, Thou whose delights are to be with the sons of men.

O Lord, how worthy art Thou to be loved, who hast done such things for love of us. I will love Thee, then, O Lord, my strength, my refuge, and my Redeemer.

O God! O Love! He that abideth in love abideth in Thee. I desire to receive Thee in this Sacrament, that I may be more firmly knit to Thee by the bonds of love. Who shall separate me from the love of Christ my Saviour? Let neither death, nor life, nor any other thing, ever separate me from the love of God, which is in Christ Jesus our Lord.

6. HUMILITY.—But how can I dare to come to Thee? Art not Thou, O Lord, my God, my Creator, the King of heaven and earth? And who am I? A vile worm of the earth, dust and ashes, nay, what is still more shameful, a sinner, often faithless and ungrateful to Thee. Truly, O Lord, I am not worthy that Thou shouldst come under my roof. But remember, Lord, that being Lord of all, Thou didst take upon Thee the form of a servant, and didst come to us, and didst treat familiarly with publicans and sinners, and at last Thou didst humble Thyself even unto death. I beseech Thee, then, let that humility move Thee not to despise me, vile and humble, but graciously come to me, or vouchsafe to receive me coming to Thee.

7. PETITION FOR GRACE.—O Father eternal,

by the merits of Thy Son, grant me grace worthily to receive, not the Sacrament only, but the very reality and the virtue of the Sacrament. I offer to Thee the lowliness and sanctity of the glorious ever Virgin Mary, with the fervour and devotion of all the saints, that their merits may supply what my feebleness is lacking in.

O Lord Jesus, be favourable to me, a sinner, and grant me so worthily to receive the mysteries of Thy Body and Blood, that I may reap plenteous fruit therefrom, and get strength against all the wiles of the world, the flesh, and the devil. May I be especially delivered from the vice of N., and fortified in every virtue required by my state, in charity, humility, and purity, so as faithfully to serve Thee all my days.

O God the Holy Ghost, let Thy power be present to me, purging my heart, and making ready in me a dwelling-place for Christ the Lord, as in the Blessed Virgin Mary.

O most holy Virgin Mary, who by the overshadowing of the Holy Ghost didst conceive and carry in thy most chaste womb God and Man, obtain for me to receive Him worthily in this Sacrament, that so I may partake of the Spirit of this thy beloved Son.

O all ye Saints of God, and ye especially my dear patrons, come to my aid with your prayers before God, that I may now receive Him in Sacrament, and one day see Him with you in glory. Amen, Amen.

SUNDAY.—AFTER COMMUNION.

8. ADORATION AND PRAISE.—O Jesus, sweetest Guest, welcome to my poor cottage. Happy is Thy visit to Thy poor and lowly servant, O Thou most Blessed One, coming into my heart from on high. O King of peace, banish from my mind and heart every vain thought, that my soul may gaze with love on Thee alone, the Author of peace. What besides Thee, O Peace and sweet Repose of my heart, does my soul seek or relish?

O Fountain of Love never decaying, how can I ever forget Thee, when Thou hast vouchsafed to remember me and to give me Thyself? Thou hast dealt mercifully with Thy servant, far beyond all I hoped for. Far above my desert hast Thou shown favour and friendship to me. What reward shall I render to Thee for this Thy grace?

O that I could only serve Thee faithfully all the days of my life. O if I could but one day give Thee a worthy service. Truly Thou art worthy of all honour and of eternal praise. Thou art my Lord, and I Thy poor servant, who am bound with my whole strength to serve Thee, never tiring of Thy praise. This is my wish, this is my desire. Fill Thou up that in which I am lacking.

Grant me Thy grace, gracious Jesus, to be with me, and to work with me, and to persevere with me to the end. Grant me ever to desire and will what is most agreeable and dearest to Thee. Let Thy will be mine, and let my will ever follow Thine, and excellently agree with it. Let me will or not will with Thee, and not be able to will or nill, but as Thou willest and nillest.

Give me to die to all that is in the world, and for Thy sake to love to be despised and unknown in this world. Give above all desired things to rest in Thee, and that my heart be at peace in Thee. Thou art the true peace of the heart, Thou its only rest. Out of Thee all things are hard and uneasy. Together with this peace that is in Thee alone, the sovereign and eternal good, will I sleep and rest. Amen.

9. THANKSGIVING.—What shall I render to Thee, O Lord Jesus, for all that Thou hast given to me, especially this day? Thou hast given me graciously Thy Body to eat and Thy Blood to drink as a pledge of glory to come. Who ever heard such a thing? who ever saw the like? Let my lips be opened and my mouth be filled with Thy praise, that I may sing of Thy glory and Thy greatness all the day long, and may tell of all Thy wondrous works.

Let my soul magnify the Lord for so many and such great benefits, and let my spirit rejoice in God my Saviour. For He hath regarded the lowness of His servant, and He that is mighty hath done for me great things. He hath filled the hungry with good things. Praise the Lord all ye Gentiles, praise Him all ye peoples, for His mercy is established upon me. Praise Him all ye His angels, praise Him all His powers, kings of the earth and all people, princes and judges of the world, young men and maidens, old men and children.

My tongue, too, tender Jesus, shall speak of Thy justice and of Thy praise all the day long. All my bones shall say, "Lord, who is like unto Thee? Thou art mighty, O Lord, and Thy truth standeth fast, magnificent in Thy gifts, and holy in all Thy works. Let my speech be pleasing in Thy sight. All my delight is in Thee, and I will exercise myself in Thy commandments. Hold me by my right hand, and guide me by Thy will, and afterwards receive me in glory. Amen.

10. OBLATION OF CHRIST.—Most gracious God, who hast so loved me as to give me Thine Only-begotten Son for my meat and drink, and with Him all things, look now upon the Face of Thy Christ, in whom Thou art well pleased. I offer to Thee this Thy Beloved Son, and with Him my own heart, for all that Thou hast given me this day. Be pleased, Father, with this oblation, and through Him turn Thine indignation from me.

Behold, it is Jesus Christ, the Mediator between God and man, who now intercedes for me, my advocate and high priest. Him do I present unto Thee, who has done no sin, who has taken away the sins of the world, by whose stripes our sicknesses are healed. Receive, Holy Father, this spotless Victim, to the praise and glory of Thy name, in thanksgiving for all benefits by me received, as an atonement for my sins, and to supply all my shortcomings.

11. OBLATION OF SELF.—O Lord, seeing that I am Thy servant and the child of Thy handmaid, I renounce Satan, and all his works, and all his pomps. Thou alone art the God of my heart and my portion for ever. Thou art the portion of my inheritance, and of my cup. Thou shalt restore my inheritance to me. Take, then, all that I have free, my memory, my understanding, and all my will. Whatever I have Thou hast given me. To Thee I restore the whole again, to be entirely governed by Thy will. Give me only Thy love and Thy grace, and I am rich enough; I ask for nothing more.—*S. Ignatius.*

12. PETITION.— O Almighty, everlasting God, keeper of souls and Redeemer of the world, graciously look on me Thy servant, bowed down before the feet of Thy Divine Majesty. Accept this Sacrifice of the Mass to the glory of Thy Name, for the salvation of the living and the dead, and especially for the remission of my own sins. Turn Thine anger from me, grant me grace and mercy, rid me from every evil, and open to me the gate of paradise. Grant me thus faithfully to persevere to the end, and join me with the flock of Thy elect, through Thy grace, O my God, to whose Name be blessing, honour, and dominion for ever and ever. Amen.

O Lord, who blessest them that bless Thee, and sanctifiest them that trust in Thee, save Thy people and bless Thine inheritance, fill up the fulness of Thy Church, sanctify them that love the beauty of Thy house, give glory to them by Thy power, and forsake not them who trust in Thee. Give to the sick succour, healing, and comfort; to travellers rest; and bless the fruits of the earth. Keep in good peace the world, the Church, kings, priests, and all Thy people. Remember those who have presented Thee with gifts, and those for whom they were presented. Console the sorrowful and distressed. Give to the living the help of Thy grace, and to the dead eternal rest, O Lord.

13. PRAYER TO B. V. MARY.—O most worshipful Queen of the world, Mother of our Lord Jesus Christ, holy Virgin Mary, who in thy sacred womb didst bear the Creator of all things, intercede for me a wretched sinner, that whatsoever negligence or irreverence I may have been guilty of in the receiving of this Sacrament may be mercifully pardoned through thy prayers.

14. To THE SAINTS.—O all ye Saints of God, who so served our Lord when living in the flesh as to merit a share in the power of His eternal kingdom, assist me, I beseech you, by your prayers, that this heavenly Bread which I have received may fortify me against all weakness, and shield me from all danger, so that in the strength of this meat I may walk safe through the desert of this world, till I reach the mountain of God, to share with you the joys that never end. Amen.

15. Conclusion.—Soul of Christ, sanctify me; Body of Christ, save me; water from Christ's side, wash me; Passion of Christ, comfort me; O good Jesus, graciously hear me; in Thy wounds hide me; never let me be parted from Thee; from the wicked foe defend me; in the hour of death call me, and bid me come to Thee, that with Thy Saints I may praise Thee for ever and ever. Amen.

MONDAY.—BEFORE COMMUNION.

16. Invocation.—Come, Holy Ghost, and fill the hearts of Thy faithful people, and kindle in them the fire of Thy love.

℣. Send forth Thy Spirit, and they shall be created.

℟. And Thou shalt renew the face of the earth.

O God, who by the light of Thy Holy Spirit didst teach the hearts of Thy faithful people, grant us by the same Spirit to have a right understanding in all things, and evermore to rejoice in His holy consolations, through Christ our Lord.

17. Contrition.—O Lord my God, be merciful to me a sinner. I am sorry for my sins; I desire to amend. Blot out all my iniquities, I beseech Thee, that with pure mind and body I may be able to go unto the Holy of Holies.

18. Faith.—O Lord Jesus Christ, who art a Priest for ever, and who hast said, "*My Flesh*

is meat indeed, and My Blood is drink indeed," I believe that Thou art Christ the Son of the Living God, who camest into this world, and art present in this Sacrament. Lord, increase my faith.

19. HOPE.—In Thee only, most sweet Jesus, do I place all my hope, for Thou art my salvation and my strength. Thou art my refuge and the spring of all my good. Save me, for Thou never forsakest those that hope in Thee.

20. CHARITY.—O how vehement was the love of Thy Heart, most blessed Jesus, which made Thee, when leaving this world, prepare for us a table with every delight, and every savour of sweetness. Therefore do I love Thee, O my God, and will never cease to love Thee. Feed my love with Thyself, for Thou art indeed the food of love.

21. DESIRE.—As the hart panteth for the fountains of water, so panteth my soul after Thee, my Saviour, Lord Jesus. Draw me to Thee, and it is enough, for beside Thee no consolation avails anything, without Thee I can have no being, without Thee I desire not to live.

22. HUMILITY.—O infinite, most mighty, and incomprehensible God, who art Thou, and who am I, that Thou vouchsafest to come and sup with me, and make Thy dwelling in me? Lord, I am not worthy that Thou shouldst come under my roof, but speak the word only, and my soul shall be healed.

23. INTENTION.—O Lord Jesus Christ, I offer Thee on the altar in union with that divine

intention with which Thou, at the last supper, and on the altar of the cross, didst offer Thyself. Be pleased, O Lord, to accept this sacrifice, and may it bring forth to us the fruit of life eternal.

24. PETITION.—I beseech Thee, O Lord Jesus Christ, for all in any way tied to me by blood, by spiritual relationship, or by friendship; for all who have done me good, who pray for me, or have asked my prayers. I pray for the whole Catholic Church, and especially for this diocese, for the Pope, the bishops, and clergy, and all Thy people, that they may persevere in Thy service, in holiness and devotion. Have mercy on all that are in trouble or distress, giving grace to the living, and eternal rest to the faithful departed. Amen.

25. ENTREATY.—To the table of Thy most sweet banquet, Lord Jesus Christ, I, a sinner, approach with trembling and fear, not presuming on my own merits, but in Thy bountiful grace and mercy. My heart and body are defiled with sin, my mind and my tongue I have not strictly kept. Therefore, O dread Majesty, yet gracious God, in my straits I run to Thee, as one miserable to the fountain of mercy; to Thee I make haste to be cured; to Thee I fly for protection, hoping to find in Thee a Saviour, whom I cannot bear as a Judge; to Thee, O Lord, I show my sores; before Thee I uncover my shame. I know that my sins are many and great, and I am afraid; but I trust in Thy mercies, which are without number. Look on me, then, Lord Jesus Christ, with the eyes of Thy mercy, O ever-

lasting King, O God and Man, crucified for the sake of men. Graciously hear me, trusting in Thee; have mercy on me, full of miseries and sin, O Thou never-failing fount of compassion.

Hail, Saving Victim, offered on the rood for me and all mankind. Hail, noble and precious Blood, flowing from the Wounds of my crucified Lord, and washing away the sins of the whole world. Remember, O Lord, Thy creatures, whom Thou hast redeemed with Thy Blood. I am grieved for having sinned, and I hope to amend. Take away my iniquities, I beseech Thee, and all my sins, that purged in mind and body, I may be made worthy to taste this banquet of the Holy of Holies, and grant that this sacred feast of Thy Body and Blood, which I unworthy am about to receive, may blot out my sins, and make me wholly clean from imperfections; may banish all foul imaginations, and renew me in good thoughts; may stir me up to all such works as please Thee, and be to me a firm defence against all the wiles of my enemies, whether of body or soul. Amen.—*S. Ambrose.*

26. To the Blessed Virgin.—Through thee let us find access to thy Son, O Blessed Virgin Mary, thou finder of grace, thou Mother of life and of salvation. May He receive us through thee, who through thee was given unto us. May thy perfect integrity excuse the fault of our corruption, and thy lowliness, so dear to God, obtain pardon for our pride and vanity. May the plenteousness of thy charity cover the multitude of

our sins, and thy glorious fruitfulness make us fruitful in deserts. O thou, our Blessed Lady, our advocate and intercessor, reconcile us to thy Son, commend us to thy Son, place our wants before thy Son. Obtain, O blessed one, by the grace which thou hast found, by the station to which thou art exalted, by the mercy to which thou hast given birth, that He who through thee became a sharer of our weakness and misery, may likewise through thee make us sharers of His bliss and glory, Jesus Christ, thy Son, our Lord, who is over all, God, blessed for ever. Amen.—*S. Bernard.*

27. To the Saints.—O all ye citizens of my heavenly country, succour my weakness, strengthen my faith and hope, kindle in me some spark of the fire of your love, clothe me in the marriage garment, give me of the plenty of your adornments, that without shame I may enter the place of the admirable tabernacle, into the heavenly banquet hall, before the majesty of God. Amen.

MONDAY.—AFTER MASS.

28. Devout Affections.—Behold now, O Lord, I have Thee, who hast all things; I possess Thee, who possessest all things. Take, then, O my God and my all, take my heart away from all that is out of Thee, in which there is only vanity and affliction of spirit. Let my heart be firmly

fixed in Thee. Be Thou its rest, for in Thee is its treasure, the sovereign truth, true and everlasting bliss.

My Jesus, let my mind feel the sweetness of Thy presence. Let it taste how delicious Thou art, that, fed with Thy love, it may seek no joy out of Thee, for Thou, O God, art the joy of my heart, and my portion for ever.

Thou art the Physician of our souls, who hast healed our sicknesses by Thy stripes. I am that sick man whom Thou camest from heaven to cure; heal, then, my soul, for I have sinned against Thee. Thou art the Good Shepherd who hast laid down Thy life for Thy sheep, and I am the sheep that was lost, yet Thou hast taken me back to Thy fold on Thy shoulders, and hast vouchsafed to feed me with Thy own Body and Blood in the pastures of comfort. What canst Thou refuse me, when Thou hast given me Thyself? Be Thou ever my Shepherd, and I shall want nothing till I be brought to the pastures of life everlasting.

O Thou true Light, which enlightenest every man that cometh into this world, give light to mine eyes that I may never sleep in the death of sin.

O Fire ever burning and never decaying, behold me, lukewarm and cold, and kindle my reins and heart, that they may burn with love of Thee; for Thou didst come to send a fire on the earth, and what wilt Thou but that it be enkindled?

O King of heaven and earth, rich in mercy,

behold me needy and poor. Thou knowest what I lack; Thou alone canst enrich and aid me. Help me, my God, and out of the treasures of Thy goodness succour my destitute soul.

My Lord and my God, behold I am Thy servant. Give me understanding that I may know Thy will, and a willing heart to perform it.

Thou art the Lamb of God, the Lamb without spot, that takest away the sins of the world; take from me all that is hurtful to me and displeasing to Thee, and give me what Thou lovest and what is profitable. Thou art my love and all my joy, my God and my all, the portion of my inheritance and of my cup.

My God and my all, let Thy most sweet love so vehemently inflame and swallow me up, that for love of Thy love I may die to the world, who for love of me didst vouchsafe to die on the cross, O my God and my all. Amen.

29. THANKSGIVING AND OBLATION.—O infinite goodness, who am I that Thou shouldst have been pleased to admit me to the sacred table of this most holy Sacrifice? Whence is it that I have so found favour in Thy sight? Come hither and hearken, all ye Angels and Saints, and I will tell you what God hath done for my soul. For me, that was the least in my Father's house, He hath raised from the dust, and hath set me with the princes of His people, that I should eat bread at His own table all the days of my life. What thanks enough can I render unto the Lord for all the benefits that He hath done unto me? Truly

is it said, "*If a man would give all the substance of his house for love, he would despise it as nothing.*"

Thou hast given me all Thou hast, Thy Body, Soul, and Godhead, and if I give Thee all the substance of my house, my body, soul, and all that I have or am, yet it is as nothing compared with Thy immense inestimable gift. I owe Thee an infinite gift like Thyself, so that I can never pay my debt. Still I beg Thy acceptance of this little present, which I offer Thee in the simplicity of my heart, saying with the spouse, "*My Beloved to me, and I to Him.*" For as Thou hast given Thyself wholly to me to be the food of my soul, so I consecrate myself wholly to Thy service, all that I have, or am, or can do, all I give to Thee; claim me as Thine own, and allow not anything to remain mine.

30. PETITIONS.—Grant me, I beseech Thee, merciful God, ardently to long after what pleaseth Thee, prudently to search into it, truly to know it, and perfectly to fulfil it.

To the praise and glory of Thy Name order Thou all my state. What Thou askest of me give me to know, and also to be able and willing to do; and may I so do it as I ought, and as shall help to my salvation. Let my way to Thee be safe and straight, so that I fail not of it either in prosperity or adversity, giving Thee thanks for the one, and being patient in the other. Let me rejoice only in what draws to Thee, and grieve only for what separates from Thee. Let me not care for pleasing or displeasing any one but Thee.

Let me do all from love, and esteem all unprofitable that tends not to Thee, and be Thou my God, dearer to me than all else. May toil for Thee be my delight, and all pleasure a weariness out of Thee.

Give me grace frequently to raise my soul to Thee, bewailing my shortcomings, and purposing to be better.

Make me, O Lord, humble without dejection, cheerful without lightness, grave without sadness, courageous without presumption, and fearing without despondency.

Make me modestly chaste, simply truthful, meekly obedient, and unrepiningly patient. Give me grace to correct my neighbour without passion, and to edify him by word and example without being lifted up.

O sweetest Jesus, let my heart be so watchful as never by one curious thought to stray from Thee. Fix it so immoveably as not to be drawn down by any unworthy affection. Give it an unconquerable courage that no stress of tribulation can weary out. Let it be so free as to be ensnared by no evil delight, how violent soever. Make it so upright as never to go aside by a crooked intention.

Give me, O my God, an understanding to know Thee, earnestness to seek Thee, and wisdom to find Thee. Give me conduct that pleases Thee, perseverance to wait for Thee, and confidence to embrace Thee. Make me repentant by Thy punishments, fruitful in good works by Thy grace, and a sharer of Thy joys by glory. Amen. —*S. Thomas Aquinas.*

31. PETITIONS FOR OTHERS.—O Lord, who blessest them that bless Thee, and sanctifiest them that trust in Thee, save Thy people and bless Thine inheritance, and keep Thy whole Church in peace. Give health to the sickly, safety to travellers, and fruitful seasons to all Thy people. Preserve the world in peace, succour those who are in distress, be beneficent to the charitable, and give eternal rest to the faithful departed. Remember, O Lord, for good all those who offer unto Thee sacrifices and gifts, and fulfil their desires, and give to them what they ask of Thee. Let the most powerful intercession of the Ever-blessed Virgin, Mother of God, prevail with Thee to be gracious to us all. Receive also the intercession of the glorious prince S. Michael the Archangel, with that of all the angelic host, the prayers of the patriarchs, prophets, apostles, martyrs, confessors, virgins, and all Thine elect, and may they draw down Thy blessing upon us for ever and ever. Amen.

32. CONCLUSION.—O Almighty and Everlasting God, Creator and Redeemer of my soul, look graciously on me Thy servant, prostrate before the feet of Thy Divine Majesty, and accept this holy Sacrifice of Thy Body and Blood for the glory of Thy Name, and for the salvation of Thy faithful ones, both living and dead. For Thy

Christ's sake turn Thine anger from me, and forgive me my offences. Deliver me from every evil which I have deserved, and open to me the gates of paradise. Make me for the future to cleave close to Thee, following the way of Thy commandments, that persevering until death, I may receive the reward of Thine elect, O my God, to whom be glory and honour, might, majesty, and dominion for ever and ever. Amen.

TUESDAY.—
BEFORE COMMUNION.

33. THANKSGIVING.—Most Blessed Saviour, Jesus Christ, I adore Thee with all my heart, and from the bottom of my soul I give Thee thanks for that with such charity Thou didst redeem us forlorn and lost, at the cost of Thy Blood; and because in memory of this Thy love, as well as for a pledge of the glory to come, Thou hast, with such admirable power, wisdom, and goodness bestowed that self-same Body and Blood upon us, to be our meat and drink in this wonderful Sacrament.

34. CONFESSION.—But alas! wretch and sinner that I am! Alas! that I have so often offended Thee by my transgressions, especially N. and N. Now, however, I grieve from my inmost heart for these my offences, and from henceforth I resolve to serve Thee alone, and to cleave wholly to Thy good pleasure.

35. Oblation.—As, then, I am now about to approach to Thy banquet table, I desire to offer to Thy Father this most worthy Sacrifice of Thy most holy Body and Blood. I offer it with the same intention with which Thou didst once offer it for us on the altar of the cross, to the glory of Thy Divine Majesty, in memory of Thy holy Incarnation, Thy bitter Passion and Death. I offer it as a great thanksgiving for all the benefits bestowed on myself and on all Thy chosen ones; as a full atonement for my sins, and those of all the world. I offer it especially for my own friends N. and N., that it may please Thee to grant them what they stand in need of; and may this Sacrifice bring relief to the dead, especially to N. and N.

36. Faith.—O my Jesus, I believe with my heart, and I confess with my mouth, that the Eternal Father, the sovereign Creator of all things, who needeth nothing, so loved the world that He gave Thee, His Only-begotten Son, to us as our Saviour. And I believe that Thou, equal in all things to Thy Father, didst out of the immensity of Thy charity, come down from the bosom of Thy Father into the womb of the Virgin Thy Mother, and wast there made Man for our salvation. I believe, also, that when instituting at the last supper the Sacrament of Thy Body and Blood, Thou didst thus give Thyself to us to be our Food, to dwell with us and we with Thee.

37. Hope.—Since, then, Thou hast beyond all

our desert dealt so lovingly with us, I come to Thee with full hope and confidence. For what canst Thou refuse to us, who hast made over to us even Thine own self?

38. LOVE.—O my good Jesus, how I love Thee for all that Thou hast done. With my whole heart I love Thee. Never let me be so foolish as to part with Thy love.

39. OBLATION.—But what shall I render to the Lord for so great a gift, and for all that He has given unto me? Behold, I renounce for Thee myself, my body and soul, and all that I have. But, after all, what have I that I have not received? and indeed what is man compared with his Maker? A vile creature, a worm of the earth, a wretched sinner, an unprofitable servant, and what can he do for God, his Lord and Creator? I see how poor and needy I am, and I humble myself under Thy mighty hand. Do Thou, however, O Lord Jesus, my Advocate and Mediator, take up my sad case, and out of the treasury of Thy immense charity aid my destitution. Represent to the Eternal Father the price of Thy merits and Thy Blood, and so supply all my shortcomings, and especially this poor preparation with which I now come to Thy tremendous mysteries, that through Thy fulness my imperfect service may find acceptance.

40. PETITIONS.—Make me also, O blessed Jesu, make me, by Thy great loving-kindness, ever with due faith, reverence, and thankful worship to receive this wonderful gift of Thy love

with a heart burning and inflamed, and adorn my soul with the choicest of Thy graces, with charity and chastity, with humility and patience, with meekness and sobriety. And I beseech Thee, that by the virtue of this Thy holy Body and Blood, my heart may be set free from all hurtful affections, and from all things that hinder the full effect of this Sacrament; that I may be intimately united and incorporated with Thee; that I may taste how sweet Thou art, and may become one spirit with Thee, that I may so dwell in Thee and Thou in me, that nothing may be able to part me from Thee. For I know how good a thing it is for me to cleave close to Thee. For what is there in heaven, or what upon earth, that I desire out of Thee? Thou art my God and my portion for ever.

41. INVOCATION OF SAINTS.—To you also do I fly for refuge, O ye Saints and friends of God, and to thee above all others, Virgin Mother, who, full of grace, didst in thy chaste womb bear Him who is God-Man. I come to you also, my patrons N. and N., most dearly beloved. You see Him face to face whom I only see in a glass darkly: you eat that manna with full relish which I only receive hidden with the veil of the species. Obtain for me so to eat of this heavenly bread during my pilgrimage through life, that together with you I may in my true home be one day satisfied with the plenitude of its sweetness.

TUESDAY.—AFTER COMMUNION.

42. **Rejoicing in the Lord.**—I have found Him whom my soul loveth, I hold Him, and will not let Him go. Thee, my Jesus, do I embrace, my love and my joy. Thee, the treasure of my heart, I clasp, in whom I possess all things. Deliver me, O Lord, from all my necessities, and make me fully Thine, as Thou art mine. Thou, O Jesus, hast made and fashioned me; create, then, in me a clean heart, and renew a right spirit within me. Thou art my Lord and my King, claim me as Thy right, and let no one possess me but Thyself. Thou art my advocate with the Father, turn Thou His anger from me. Thou art He that shalt come to judge the living and the dead; enter not into judgment with Thy servant. Thou art the Bridegroom of my soul, espouse me to Thyself in mercy and in faith. Thou art my defender, keep me close to Thee, and I care not whose hand shall fight against me. Thou art my Saviour and Redeemer, perfect the work Thou hast begun, and let not Thy labour be in vain. Thou art the portion of my lot in the land of the living, restore Thou my inheritance to me. Thou art my glory and my crown, and my reward exceeding great; admit me to those good things which Thou hast prepared for them that love Thee. O Jesus, O most kind Jesus, O Jesus, Son of the Virgin Mary, pour into me grace, wisdom, and charity, that I may perfectly love

Thee, praise Thee, enjoy Thee, and magnify Thy holy name now and for ever. Amen.

43. EXCLAMATIONS.—How beautiful art Thou, my Beloved, the Beloved of my vows, how beautiful and altogether lovely. O my only delight, my joy, my life, and sovereign sweetness. O my God and my all, after Thee I sigh, I cry. I clasp Thee with all the affections of my heart, for Thou art infinite power, wisdom past finding out, goodness itself, eternal love, complete perfection. What shall separate me from Thy charity? A momentary pleasure, or vain honours, or perishable riches? No, for it is good for me, blessed Jesus, to cleave fast to Thee, and to put all my trust in the Lord my God. Help me, my Jesus, in this my holy purpose, and never let me be so foolish as to turn away from Thee. Let this most holy Sacrament heal all my wounds, and brace me with the strength of every virtue. Let it be to me a strong defence against every danger, and a firm bulwark of life everlasting. Amen.

44. THANKSGIVING.—O gentlest Saviour Jesus Christ, how sweet and mild art Thou, and of plenteous mercy to them that call upon Thee. For when we were not, Thou didst create us by Thy divine power; and when we were Thine enemies Thou didst descend from heaven and with a marvellous wisdom didst redeem us; and since without Thee we can neither move nor be, in body or soul, Thou hast surrounded us with helps and graces, nay, Thou hast even given to

us Thy own Body and Blood, Thy very Self in this Sacrament. O love! O love! O new and stupendous mystery!

Dost Thou, then, my God, vouchsafe to come to me? the Lord of sovereign majesty to an abject slave? God to man, the Creator to the creature? Whence is this to me, that my Lord should come to me? O Lord our God, how admirable is Thy Name in all the earth. Who can tell of all Thy might, or who relate all Thy praises? If I had the tongues of men and of angels, if each breath I drew were an act of thanksgiving, yet should I fall short of worthily confessing Thy mercies. What, then, can I do for my insufficiency, but call on all creation to bless and praise Thy name to everlasting?

45. OBLATION.—O Father of mercies and God of all consolation, who through the abundance of Thy charity hast given to me Thine Only-begotten Son through the Sacrament of His Body and Blood, behold now I present Him unto Thee closely united with myself, as my own possession, and I offer Him to Thee in union with that love with which He offered Himself at the last supper and on the altar of the cross. Lo! this is my treasure, merciful Father. In this treasure I put all my trust. These are the riches which I offer for the payment of my great debts.

Look, O tender Father, look upon the face of Thy Christ. It is Thy own beloved Son in whom Thou art well pleased. See how He is now intimately joined with me, and for His sake I beseech Thee to look also upon me with an eye of pity. Under His protection and guardianship, under the shadow of His merits, I dare to appear before Thee, that when Thou lookest on Him Thou mayest with Him behold also me with kindness His servant for ever.

Do not let that soul perish which so often lodges the Lord, who was sent by Thee to seek and to save that which was lost, but spare me for Thy mercy's sake. Amen.

46. SUPPLICATIONS.—I beseech Thee, O my God, that the Saving Victim offered for me in these holy mysteries may fully blot out my sins and those of the whole world; and by this Communion be pleased to restore in me what has been ruined by transgression. Supply all that is wanting to me, destroy what displeases Thee, and make of me a chosen vessel, one after Thine own Heart. Make me to grow up into the image of Thy Son, subjecting me, body, soul, and spirit, unto Him, that I may be myself no longer, but may be wholly transmuted into Him, to the glory of Thy Name.

Convert, O Lord, all sinners, and bring back to the Church all that are in heresy or schism. Enlighten unbelievers, assist all that are in distress, be gracious to all who have been commended to my prayers, to all my relations, friends, and benefactors, both living and dead. Give Thou to the living pardon and grace, and to the faithful departed rest and light everlasting.

47. PRAYER TO MARY.—O most holy Virgin

Mother, behold I have received thy beloved Son, whom thou didst conceive in thy spotless womb, whom thou didst bring forth, and to whom thou gavest milk, whom thou didst clasp in thy chaste embrace. Behold with lowly love I present Him whose sight gladdened thee and filled thee with delight, and I offer Him in thy most pure arms to the Most Holy Trinity as an act of sovereign worship for thy honour and glory, and the needs of myself and of all the world. Thou hast a Mother's power with God, and thy petitions are never refused. Let, then, the power thou hast be mercifully made known to the world by obtaining by thy prayers pardon for the guilty, health for the sick, courage for the faint of heart, comfort for the afflicted, and help for those in danger. Amen.

48. To THE SAINTS.—O all ye Saints of God, the comfort of my soul, especially you my patrons and protectors, behold your Master is within me, from whom you derive all your sanctity. Obtain for me from Him, whose example you so faithfully copied, that I may follow in your footsteps, and so arriving at perfection may, full of merits, be worthy of your blessed company.

49. CONCLUSION.—I leave Thee, my Jesus, for a little while, but I take Thee also with me, Thou who art my comfort, my happiness, and all the good of my soul. To Thy most loving Heart I commend myself, my friends, and my enemies. Love us, O Lord, and transform us closely into

Thy likeness. May I be wholly occupied in Thee and for Thee. May I have no object in all my words and actions but Thy glory and profit, O Love of my soul, who livest and reignest world without end. Amen.

WEDNESDAY.—
BEFORE COMMUNION.

50. INTENTION.—O Lord my God, I, Thine unworthy servant, desire this morning to offer this sacrifice of the Body and Blood of Thy Son, with the greatest reverence and devotion, in union with that same sacrifice which our Lord Jesus Christ offered at the last supper, and finished on the altar of the cross, Himself both Priest and Victim. I offer it with the same dispositions as He then offered Himself, together with the merits of the glorious Virgin Mary and all the Saints, for the pure love of Thee, and with the wish that Thy good pleasure may in all things be accomplished.

I offer it as an acknowledgment of Thy sovereign power over all creatures, and of our complete dependence on Thee, and subjection to Thee, in thanksgiving for all Thy benefits bestowed on all Thy creatures, as an atonement for all the wrongs done to Thy Divine Majesty, to increase the joy of our Lord Jesus Christ, and the glory and beatitude of the most holy Virgin, and all the Saints.

I offer it as a satisfaction for all my sins, and to procure for my body and soul all that I now or hereafter may require; I offer it, lastly, for all the living and dead, for whom I am bound to pray, for my relations, friends, and benefactors; for the welfare of the Catholic Church, the peace of Christian princes, the rooting out of heresies, the conversion of unbelievers, the advancement in holiness of the clergy and Religious persons, and for the souls in purgatory, especially N. and N.

Receive, O Lord, these prayers of Thy unworthy servant, and give me grace to persevere in all that is good, even to the end. Amen.

51. ACTS OF VIRTUES.—I believe in Thee, my God, who art the very truth, who canst neither deceive nor be deceived, I adore Thee as my beginning and last end. I hope in Thee because of the abundance of Thy mercies, and I love Thee because Thou art goodness itself. I am confounded and blush to think that I have preferred vanities before Thee the infinite Good. I grieve for my sins, and I purpose to amend and to do satisfaction and penance; and I thank Thee for the multitude of those benefits which Thou hast heaped upon me in such rich overflow. Whatsoever I possess I give back to Thy Hand, to be entirely disposed of by Thee. All that have offended me, I forgive from the bottom of my heart. And I beseech Thee, by the bitter Passion

of Thy Son, to be gracious to my poor soul. O my Jesus, visit me now with Thy salvation when Thou enterest within me. Abide with me, and let my soul come to Thee in its last passage, fortified with the sacraments and with every help to life eternal. Amen.

52. SUPPLICATION.—Almighty, Eternal God, behold I approach to the Sacrament of Thy Only-begotten Son Jesus Christ. I approach as one sick to the Physician of life, as one unclean to the fountain of mercy, as one blind to the light of eternal glory, as poor and needy to the Lord of heaven and earth. I ask Thee, then, out of the plenteousness of Thy mercy, to heal my sickness, to wash away my filthiness, to enlighten my blindness, to enrich my poverty, and to clothe my nakedness, that with such reverence, devotion, humility, and contrition, such purity, faith, purpose, and intention, I may receive this Bread of angels, the King of kings and Lord of lords, as is expedient for the health of my soul. Give me, I beseech Thee, not only to receive the outward Sacrament of the Lord's Body and Blood, but also the reality and virtue of the Sacrament. Give me, O Lord, so to receive that Body of our Lord Jesus Christ, which He took from the Virgin Mary, that I may be thereby mystically incorporated with His Body, and counted amongst His members. O tender Father, give me also one day to behold for ever with open face Thy beloved Son, whom now I propose to receive under the veils of the species, who liveth and

reigneth with Thee, in the unity of the Holy Spirit for ever and ever. Amen.—*S. Thomas Aquinas.*

53. TO THE BLESSED VIRGIN.—O Mother of pity, most blessed Virgin Mary, I, a miserable sinner, fly to thee for refuge, beseeching of thee that as thou didst assist beneath the cross, so thou mayest be with me, receiving the memorial of thy Son's Passion, that it may, by thy prayers, be more profitable to my soul.

54. TO THE SAINTS.—And you, O Saints of God, whose memory we celebrate this day on earth, I offer this Communion to increase your glory and happiness, begging you to intercede for me, that my service may be acceptable to my God, and that one day I may be admitted to praise Him for ever in the courts above. Amen.

WEDNESDAY.—
AFTER COMMUNION.

55. O Godhead hid, devoutly I adore Thee,
    Who truly art within the forms before me;
    To Thee my heart I bow, with bended knee,
    As failing quite in contemplating Thee.

    Sight, touch, and taste in Thee are each deceived,
    The ear alone most safely is believed.

I believe all the Son of God hath spoken,
Than Truth's own word there is no truer
token.

God only, on the cross, lay hid from view,
But here lies hid at once the Manhood too;
And I, in both professing my belief,
Make the same prayer as the repentant thief.

Thy Wounds, as Thomas saw, I do not see,
Yet Thee confess my Lord and God to be.
Make me believe Thee ever more and more,
In Thee my hope, in Thee my love to store.

O Thou Memorial of our Lord's own dying,
O living Bread, to mortals life supplying;
Make Thou my soul henceforth on Thee to
live,
Ever a taste of heavenly sweetness give.

O loving Pelican! O Jesu, Lord!
Unclean I am, but cleanse me in Thy Blood,
Of which a single drop for sinners spilt
Can purge the entire world from all its guilt.

Jesu, whom for the present veiled I see,
What I so thirst for, oh! vouchsafe to me,
That I may see Thy countenance unfolding,
And may be blest Thy glory in beholding.

56. THANKSGIVING.—I thank Thee, O God,
kind benefactor of my soul, for bestowing on me,
unworthy, a share in these glorious and heavenly

mysteries. But what reward shall I render unto Thee, for I am of less value than the meanest of Thy gifts? Accept, most gracious God, the praises and thanksgivings which Thy Son offered to Thee in our human nature from the first moment of His Incarnation to the very end of His life, and those especially when, at the institution of this Sacrament, He lifted up His eyes unto heaven, and gave thanks to Thee His Almighty Father.

Receive also those thanksgivings which the Mother of Thine Only-begotten Son offered to Thee when she conceived within her purest womb Him who I have now received within my breast. Receive those praises which she poured forth to Thee when she gave Thy Son birth, and those which she gave Thee for the grace of His blessed company as long as He lived, and those which after His Ascension she still paid to Thee so often, as with tenderest devotion and heartfelt joy she received Him in the Most Holy Sacrament.

May the angelic host bless and praise Thee, standing in awe before the throne of Thy majesty, and singing, Holy, Holy, Holy, Lord God of Sabaoth.

I desire also that all the saints reigning with Thee in heaven, whose communion we believe, may fill up my shortcomings by those most worthy praises which, in the use and veneration of this Sacrament on earth, they were wont to render to Thee, and which now they chant to Thee on high, eating to the full of the Bread of Life, and drinking of the torrent of Thy pleasure. Give me to share in the merits of those that fear Thee, and keep Thy commandments. And oh, that I could gather together into myself all the fervours and the vehement devotion of Thy faithful ones still on earth, all their desires and all their merits, and so love and honour Thee with heart and soul, in return for the love and honour Thou bestowest on me in feeding me in this Holy Sacrament.

57. PETITIONS.—I believe, O Lord, but let me believe more firmly. I hope, but let my hope be more assured. I love, but I would love more ardently; I grieve, but I would do so more intensely.

I adore Thee as my beginning; I desire Thee as my last end; I praise Thee as my benefactor; I call on Thee as my strong defender.

Guide me with Thy wisdom, restrain me by Thy justice, console me by Thy kindness, and protect me by Thy power.

I offer to Thee, O God, my thoughts to be directed to Thee, my words to be spoken of Thee, my actions to be done according to Thy Heart, my sufferings to be borne for Thee.

I will whatsoever Thou willest, I will because Thou willest, I will as Thou willest, and I will so long as Thou willest.

I pray Thee, O Lord, to enlighten my understanding, to inflame my will, to cleanse my body, and to hallow my soul.

Let me not be infected by pride, moved by

WEDNESDAY. 41

flattery, deceived by the world, or ensnared by Satan.

Give me grace to purify my memory, to bridle my tongue, to order my eyes, and to curb my senses.

May I weep over my past sins, repel future temptations, correct my evil bent, and adorn myself with virtue.

Give me, O good God, a love of Thee, a hatred of myself, a zeal for my neighbour, and a contempt of the world.

May I study to be obedient to my superiors, condescending to my inferiors, obliging to my friends, and hateful to no one.

Let me remember, blessed Jesus, Thy example and commandments, by loving my enemy, suffering wrongs, doing good to my persecutors, and praying for them that slander me.

May I overcome pleasure by austerity, avarice by bounty, anger by meekness, and lukewarmness by devotion.

Make me prudent in counsel, constant in dangers, patient in adversity, and humble in prosperity.

Give me grace to be attentive at prayer, sober in diet, diligent at work, and firm of purpose.

May I take care to be holy within, modest without, exemplary in my conversation, and regular in my life.

May I be watchful to subdue nature, to cherish grace, to keep the law, and to obtain salvation.

May I pursue after sanctity, by sincere confessions, fervid communions, recollection of mind, and a pure intention of heart.

Teach me, O God, the frailty of things earthly, the grandeur of things divine, the shortness of what ends with time, and the length of eternity.

Let me forestall death, be afraid of the judgment, escape hell, and obtain heaven, through Christ our Lord. Amen.—*Clement XI.*

58. SUPPLICATIONS.—O Lord, the bowels of whose mercy are open to all, who willest not that any should perish, but that all should be saved, and who hast suffered death and instituted this Sacrament for this end, give holiness to Thy priests, peace and tranquillity to princes and kingdoms, chastity to virgins, continence to all consecrated to God, a holy wedlock to the married, pardon to the repentant, perseverance to the just, forgiveness to sinners, and especially to miserable me, protection to widows and orphans, a livelihood to the poor, a safe retreat to travellers, comfort to those that mourn, and to all faithful Christians, living and dead, grace and life everlasting. Amen.—*S. Augustine.*

59. TO THE B. V. MARY.—O my Lady, holy Mary, into thy blessed keeping, and into the lap of thy loving kindness, I commend my body and soul, this day and every day, and especially at the hour of my death. All my hopes and fears, all my distresses and my joys, I put into thy hands, my life and the end of my life I commit to thee, that by thy holy intercession and merits, all may be directed and arranged

according to thy will and that of thy Son.   Amen.
—*S. Francis of Assisi.*

60. To the Saints.—O ye Saints of God, and blessed angelic spirits, whom God gladdens with the light of His countenance, disdain not to pray for me. I salute you and render you homage; I rejoice that God has prevented you with the blessings of His sweetness; obtain for me pardon, grace, and perfect union with God.

61. Conclusion.—O God, whose mercies are without number, and whose goodness is without end, we thank Thee for all the benefits bestowed upon us, beseeching Thy clemency, that as Thou hast granted our petitions, so Thou mayest bring us to the rewards of heaven, through Christ our Lord. Amen.

THURSDAY.—
BEFORE COMMUNION.

62. Wonder.—Thy voice, it is, O Lord, the Holy of Holies, saying, Come to Me, all ye that labour, and are heavy laden, and I will refresh you. Behold Thou inclinest towards me, Thou wishest to be with me, Thou invitest me to Thy banquet, Thou givest me the bread of heaven, and Angels' Food to eat, that is Thyself, the Living Bread, who camest down from heaven and givest life unto the world.

63. Praise.—O God, Thou unseen Creator of

the world, how sweetly and graciously dost Thou treat with Thy elect, to whom Thou settest forth Thyself to be taken in Sacrament. Rejoice, O my soul, and give thanks to God, for this so singular and excellent a comfort, given to Thee in this vale of tears.

64. FEAR.—My sins indeed make me afraid, and my unclean conscience strikes me back as I approach to these dread mysteries; the sweetness of Thy words invites me, but the multitude of my iniquities overwhelms me. Who am I that I should presume to draw nigh? How shall I be bold to come to Thee, who am conscious of nothing good in myself? How shall I bring Thee into my house, who have many times shown disrespect to that Face before which the Saints and Angels tremble with awe.

65. CONTRITION.—I have sinned, O Lord, I have sinned, pity and pardon me. What can I do for my sins but confess and bewail them, beseeching Thee earnestly to be appeased? Graciously hear me, I pray Thee, O my God. All my sins displease me exceedingly, I wish never to offend Thee any more, so long as I live, only forgive me, for the sake of Thy most holy Name. Behold I trust myself to Thy mercy, I resign myself into Thy Hands. Do Thou take all the transgressions I have committed from the first hour in which I was capable of sin until now, and purge away their stains in the fire of Thy love. Cleanse my conscience wholly, and

restore mercifully to the plenitude of Thy favour, by giving to me the kiss of peace.

66. FAITH.—I believe and confess that Thou, my God, the Holy of Holies, the Creator of all things, and Lord of the Angels, art present in the Sacrament of the Altar. That which I understand not I securely trust to Thee, O my God, who never deceivest. And if Thy works were easy of comprehension to human reason, they would not be called marvellous and unutterable. O how admirable is Thy power, O Lord; how mighty is Thy truth. Thou didst speak and all things were made; Thou commandedst and they stood fast.

67. HOPE.—Confiding in Thy goodness and great mercy I draw nigh, O Lord, as one sick to the Saviour, hungry and thirsty to the Fountain of Life, destitute to the King of heaven, the servant to his Lord, a creature to his Creator, desolate to my tender comforter, hoping that in this Sacrament grace may be conferred on my soul, her lost virtue may be repaired, and her beauty, disfigured by sin, may be restored, and that my whole being may be in future preserved undefiled.

68. CHARITY.—O my Beloved, grant me for Thee to leave all other beloveds, and Thee alone to love above all things, and to keep Thee as my friend, whether I live or die. To be without Thee is a grievous hell, and to be with Thee is a sweet paradise. O good treasure! O good above every good! my God and my All! To one who

understands this, enough is said, and to repeat it often is pleasant to one that loves. Purify, gladden, clear, and quicken my spirit, that it may cleave fast to Thee with all its powers.

69. DESIRE.—Behold, O Lord, in Thee is all that I can or ought to desire. Thou art my salvation and redemption, my hope and my strength, my glory and my crown. I desire now devoutly to receive Thee. I desire, with Zacheus, to bring Thee into my house, that I may get Thy blessing, and be counted among the children of Abraham. My soul and my body long for Thee, my heart desires to be united to Thee. Turn not Thy Face from me; delay not Thy visitation; take not Thy comfort away. Come, Lord, come to Thy poor servant; come and satiate me with Thy glad presence. Till I receive this I can have no full joy.

70. SUPPLICATION.—O most blessed grace, which makes the poor in spirit rich in virtue, come down upon me and fill me with thy consolation, that my soul may not faint for dryness of mind. Prevent, O Lord God, I beseech Thee, the soul of Thy servant with the blessings of Thy sweetness, that I may worthily and devoutly draw nigh to Thy most glorious Sacrament. Stir up my heart within me, and wake me from slumber. Whatever is wanting to me do Thou, good Jesus, most holy Saviour, most graciously supply. Give to Thy poor suppliant to feel at least some little sweetness of affection in the receiving of the Holy Communion, that my faith

may grow stronger, my hope become firmer, and my love more inflamed, and that, tasting of the heavenly manna, I may not faint in the way.

71. To the B. V. Mary.—O undefiled and ever-blessed incomparable Virgin Mary, Mother of God, temple of the Most High, sanctuary of the Holy Ghost, and gate of heaven, through whom, after God, the whole world has its life; incline, O Mother of mercy, the ears of thy goodness to my unworthy supplications, and be favourable to my sinful soul in every aid, and especially obtain for me the grace to receive with great fruit the sacred Communion of the Body and Blood of thy Son.

72. To the Angels and Saints.—Angels, archangels, thrones, dominations, principalities, powers, virtues, cherubim and seraphim, you also, all Saints of God, especially my beloved patrons, vouchsafe to intercede for your most lowly servant, and offer this Communion which I am about to make to the glory of God's holy Name, to my own profit, and that of all the Church. Amen.

73. Intention.—I wish to receive this Communion of the Sacred Body and Blood of my Redeemer for my own spiritual welfare, and especially to obtain the virtue and grace of N. I desire to receive it for the good of the whole Church, militant, suffering, and triumphant, especially for those who have been commended, or who have commended themselves to my prayers and good offices. May the Almighty and merci-

ful Lord give me joy and peace, amendment of life, and time for repentance, the grace and comfort of the Holy Ghost, perseverance in good works, and true contrition of heart, advancement in virtue, and a happy death. Amen.

THURSDAY.—
AFTER COMMUNION.

74. ADORATION.—O my Beloved, chosen out of thousands, in whom I desire to abide all the days of my life. O essence of peace, in whom alone is sovereign rest. O hidden God, whose speech is with the lowly. O Love immense, bestowed ineffably on my soul. O Jesus, how great is Thy sweetness in this Thy banquet! How delightful would it be to me to wash Thy feet, like pious Magdalen, with my tears. Oh, what a great Lord have I received. What a dear Guest have I taken to lodge with me. What a delightful Companion am I joined to. What a faithful Friend, what a noble Spouse do I embrace. O good Jesus, let heaven and earth be still before Thy presence. Keep thyself in secret, O my soul, and enjoy the delicious company of thy Friend; for thou hast Him now whom the whole world cannot take from thee.

75. PRAISE.—O sweetest Saviour, may all peoples, tribes, and tongues praise Thy holy and glorious Name, and magnify it with songs of

jubilation. Behold I offer to Thee all the thrilling joys of devout hearts, their spiritual affections, their ravishments of mind, supernatural illuminations, and heavenly visions; I offer them with all the praises rendered to Thee by every creature in earth and heaven. Receive my vows, O Lord my God, and the desires of praise and blessing without end. Thou dost deserve all the honour and worship and adoration that can possibly be given to Thy majesty.

76. GRATITUDE.—O kindest Jesus, O what thanks is due to Thee from poor me, for the receiving of Thy Sacrament, the value of which no man may worthily reckon up. I bless Thee, O Good Shepherd, for that Thou hast vouchsafed to feed me, a wretched exile, with the sweet food of Thy Body and Blood. What reward can I render to Thee for this grace, and for Thy excellent charity? I will give Thee my heart, for it is the only offering I can make, that it may be wholly and intimately joined to Thee. Be pleased to remain with me, for I would wish for ever to abide with Thee: this is my only desire, ever to be united with Thee.

77. OBLATION.—As then Thou, O Lord, with Thy arms stretched out on the cross, didst freely offer Thyself wholly to the Father for my sins, so that nothing remained to Thee which was not given up to appease the divine wrath, so do I offer myself, with all my strength, and with every affection of my heart, to be an oblation completely surrendered to Thee. And I ask

Thee, O Lord, in all simplicity, to accept me as a servant for ever, that all I do may be a sacrifice of perpetual praise. Receive me in union with the oblation of Thy own precious Body and Blood, which in the presence of Thy Angels in heaven, and of Thy Church upon earth, has now been offered on Thy holy altar.

78. PETITIONS.—Grant to me, O God, my Saviour, that my devotion for this Sacrament may increase with my use of it. Save my soul, which Thou hast redeemed with Thy Precious Blood. Have respect, not to my wickedness, but to Thine own goodness. What good there is in me, little as it is, be pleased to accept, and make me ever better, and spur on my sluggish soul to a good end.

O most sweet and loving Jesus, behold I stand before Thee, poor and naked, imploring Thy grace and mercy. Inflame my coldness with the fire of Thy love. Let all earthly things become to me tasteless and bitter, despised and forgotten, but be Thou to me ever more sweet and delightful. I wish to be wholly melted into Thee, transformed entirely out of myself into Thee, and made one spirit with Thee, by the grace of internal union and ardent love. Work with me this change, as Thou hast done in Thy Saints, in a marvellous manner, O Thou Fire, ever burning and never decaying, O Love, purifying all things, and filling the understanding with light.

79. FOR OTHERS.—Be pleased, O good Jesus, to receive favourably the desires of all devout

persons, to bless all my relations, my friends, and those that have done me good, who pray for me, or desire that I should pray for them, whether they be living or dead. Give to them the help of Thy grace, protection from dangers, freedom from pains, and deliverance from every evil, that they may magnify Thy holy Name.

I pray also especially for any who have injured me, hurt my feelings, or insulted me, and for those whom I at any time have injured, whether in body or soul; whom I have troubled, scandalized, or annoyed by word or deed, knowingly or ignorantly, that all our sins and mutual offences may be wholly forgiven and blotted out.

Take from our hearts, O Lord, all suspicion, indignation, and ill-feeling, such as is contrary to charity and brotherly love. Have mercy, O Lord, on all who beg Thy mercy, and make us to be such as shall be worthy of Thy grace, so that we may persevere to life eternal. Amen.

80. To THE B. V. MARY.—I commend myself to thee, holy Virgin, Queen of heaven and earth, who in thy most sacred womb didst conceive Him whom I have but now received in Sacrament, and I pray thee to intercede for me to this thy Son, that whatever fault I may have committed of negligence or unworthiness in the taking of these dread mysteries, may through thy merits be cancelled. Thou hast ever been chaste, innocent, and undefiled; purer, holier, and more pleasing to God after the conception of thy Son than even before. O that I, by the

receiving of this Sacrament, may be more holy and pure, so that henceforth my body and soul may be preserved ever free and clear from the stain of mortal sin. When thou hadst conceived by the Holy Ghost, thou didst magnify the Lord in a song of praise, and didst rejoice in God thy Saviour. Obtain for me that by the grace of this Communion I may also exult in canticles of praise, and may by my actions give high praise to that Redeemer who has been pleased to take up His lodging with His unworthy servant, that so I may be in all things a wise and faithful servant. Amen.

81. To THE SAINTS.—Happy Saints, who have passed the stormy sea of life, and are crowned now with unfading glory, look on my manifold miseries; give something to my weakly soul, that becoming stronger, I may be stout in the battle. Ye who are now safe at home, succour the exile during his weary pilgrimage. Gather round me as I rejoice in your glories, and obtain for me the grace to imitate your virtues, that one day, by your assistance, I may be a sharer in your crowns.

82. CONCLUSION.—Now dost Thou dismiss Thy servant, O Lord Jesus, in peace. Do not Thou, however, remove far from me, but be ready to help me, for there arise up against me many thoughts and temptations with great violence. Grant that I may pass onward unhurt; give me power to crush my foes; fight Thou for me, and defeat the evil beasts and slippery lusts: com-

mand the winds and the tempest; say to the sea, Be still; and to the north wind, Blow thou not; then there will be a great calm. Bless and sanctify me with Thy heavenly benediction; protect and guard the soul of Thy servant amidst all the needs of life, that by the way of peace I may arrive safe in my heavenly home. Amen.

FRIDAY.—BEFORE MASS.

83. MEMORY OF THE PASSION.—O God, who for the redemption of the world didst choose to be born, circumcised, rejected by the Jews, betrayed by Judas with a kiss, bound and led like a lamb to the slaughter, and who before Annas, Caiphas, Herod, and Pilate, wast mocked, accused by false witnesses, buffeted, scourged, spit upon, crowned with thorns, blindfolded, and struck with a reed, who at length wast stripped of Thy garments, fastened to the cross with nails, set up between two thieves, fed with gall and vinegar, and put to a cruel death. I call to mind all these Thy bitter pains, and I beseech Thee, by Thy holy cross and death, now to be commemorated on the altar, I beseech Thee to deliver me from all my sins, and to receive me as a victim in union with Thy own sacrifice, who livest and reignest with the Father and the Holy Spirit, one God, world without end. Amen.

84. CONTRITION.—O my sweetest Saviour, I

grieve from the bottom of my heart that I ever offended Thee, my Lord and my God, Thee whom I ought to love above all things, who art so good in Thyself and so good to me. Alas! wretch that I am! I have returned Thee evil for Thy good. But be merciful to me, O Lord. Now I propose never to offend Thee any more, and to avoid all occasions of sin. And I desire to receive this Sacrament that I may be strengthened in Thy love, and may surmount every temptation, abiding in Thee and Thou in me.

85. VIRTUES.—O infinite Wisdom, eternal Truth, who canst neither deceive nor be deceived, I believe in Thee, and I believe all Thou proposest to be believed by Thy Church. Especially I believe Thou art present in this Sacrament, for Thou hast so declared it to be in words that are plain and clear. I believe Thee more than my own reasonings or my senses. For this faith, through Thy grace, I am prepared to die.

O infinite Goodness, I hope in Thee, and by Thy mercies without number I trust to have pardon, and grace, and future glory.

I love Thee, and will love Thee, and I will love all Thou lovest for Thy sake, O spring of all good, who art worthy of all love.

I rejoice at the immensity of Thy perfection, Thy bliss, and Thy loveableness, and at all the laud, honour, and worship which is or ever shall be rendered to Thee by Thy elect and by all Thy creatures. I embrace all Thy will and good pleasure, and I kiss with humble reverence every token thereof.

Whatever affection I have in me to creatures, I now transfer to Thee. All that I do or suffer, may it be to Thy glory. I am Thine wholly; do with me whatsoever Thou wilt, now and for ever. Amen.

86. INTENTION.—To the praise and glory of the Holy Trinity, in memory of the Life, Passion, Death, and Resurrection of our Saviour Jesus Christ, to the honour and exaltation of the most blessed Virgin Mary, and of all the Angels and Saints, I present this oblation of the Holy Sacrifice, with all the adorations of the blessed spirits, and the prayers and good works of the whole world. I do so to obtain help for my own necessities of body and soul, either present or future; to obtain true contrition and the pardon of all my sins; for the salvation of my relations, my benefactors, my friends, and enemies; for their needs, spiritual and temporal: I present this sacrifice for the whole Catholic Church, for its conservation and increase, for peace between Christian princes, for the rooting out of heresies, for the Pope, our bishops, the clergy, and all the faithful, for all committed or commended to me, and generally for all the living and the dead in Christ, for all that are dear to God and to His holy Catholic Church. Amen.

87. TO THE HOLY GHOST.—Spirit of grace and mercy, Holy Spirit, God, behold I approach to the sacred altar. O how dreadful is this place!

Holy Spirit, come down upon me, and take away my unworthiness. Come, cleanser of the soul, healer of wounds, take away from me all that displeases Thee, the Father, or the Son. Pour into my heart Thy most excellent graces, that so adorned I may be fit to receive my Jesus, and may live according to His will.

88. To the B. V. Mary.—Most glorious Mother of God, Virgin Mary, the comfort and the hope of my soul, assist me, a wretched sinner, by thy presence, when I offer on the altar of my heart the most precious Body and Blood of thy Son, as with love and tender pity, thou didst stand by thy Son when He offered Himself for our salvation on the cross. Despise me not, Mother of Mercy, nor turn away thine eyes for the filthiness of my sins, since thy Son has so loved me as to give His life for me.

89. To the Saints.—O all ye Saints of God, who with open vision behold Him, whom we see still in a glass darkly under this Sacrament, pray for me that by its fruit I may be one day made your companion in bliss.

FRIDAY.—AFTER COMMUNION.

90. Pious Affections.—O good Jesus! what have I in heaven but Thee, and what upon earth have I desired but Thee? My longing is now accomplished, my joy is full; for in Thee

is my fulness, in Thee all my desire, and all my good. Fill my hungry soul with good things, kindle my coldness with Thy fire of love, enlighten my blindness with the glory of Thy presence. Raise up my soul above all earthly things, penetrate my inmost heart with the virtue of this sacrament, and let it kill and root out whatever is faulty or vicious. Be Thou, O my Jesus, all my delight. Let all rest be bitter to me, that is not in Thee, send a ray of Thy charity into me to burn up in me every earthly thing, and let the old man be entirely destroyed. I wish to be wholly transformed into Thee, swallowed up in Thee, and with Thee made one.

91. LOVE.—O God, I love Thee, nor do I love Thee that Thou mayest save me, nor because those that love Thee not, Thou punishest in eternal fire. Thou, my Jesus, didst embrace me wholly on the cross. Thou didst bear the nails, the lance, and much disgrace, countless sorrows, sweat, agony, and death, and these for me—for me a sinner. How then should I not love Thee, most loving Jesus, not that Thou mayest save me in heaven, nor lest Thou shouldst for ever damn me in hell, nor for hope of reward; but as Thou hast loved me, so do I, and will I love Thee, only because Thou art my King, and only because Thou art my God.—*S. Francis Xavier.*

92. THANKSGIVING.—I thank Thee, holy Lord, Almighty Father, everlasting God, who for no merits of mine, but solely by Thy own mercy,

hast vouchsafed to feed me an unworthy sinner, with the precious Body and Blood of Thy Son, our Lord Jesus Christ, and I pray that this Holy Communion may not increase my guilt, but intercede for my pardon. Let it be to me an armour of faith, and a shield of good will. May it empty me of vice, and rid me of every lust. May it increase in me charity and patience, humility and obedience, and every virtue. Let it be a defence against the wiles of every enemy, visible or invisible. Let it put to sleep all evil motions, fleshly or spiritual. Let it make me cling close to Thee, the one true God, my end and sovereign perfection. And I pray Thee to bring me, a sinner, to that banquet, where with the Son and the Spirit, Thy Saints enjoy true light, full content, everlasting gladness, complete delight, and perfect happiness, through the same Jesus Christ our Lord. Amen.—*S. Thomas Aquinas.*

93. OBLATION.—O God, my protector, behold, and look on the Face of Thy Christ. See how Thy Son has communicated Himself to me, so that He is in me, and I in Him,—He is one with me, and I with Him. Him now I offer to Thee, most loving Father, as a sweet smelling savour, for Thy own great glory, as a thanksgiving for all benefits, for the remission of my sins and those of all the world, to obtain for me all the things, temporal and spiritual, of which I or others stand in need, and for the souls of all the faithful departed. And with

this oblation receive my soul and body, all my powers and all my affections, as a perpetual holocaust burning before Thy Divine Majesty. Let me have no life or being henceforth, but to love and serve Thee. Amen.

94. REPARATION.—O my Jesus, who in this Sacrament dost suffer innumerable insults, I detest from my whole heart all the injuries thus done to Thee. Let Thy great charity appease Thy Almighty Father, and light up in my heart by Thy Sacred Presence such zeal for Thy honour, that I may bewail the profanations of Thy Sacrament, and strive to prevent them with all my power.

95. INVOCATION.—Pierce, sweetest Lord Jesus, the marrow of my soul, with the delightful and wholesome wound of Thy love; with true peaceful, and apostolic holy charity, that my soul may melt and faint away with only love and desire of Thee, longing and fainting for Thy courts, desiring to be dissolved and to be with Thee. Grant that my soul may hunger after Thee, the Bread of Angels, the repast of holy souls, our daily supersubstantial Bread, having in it all sweetness, and the savour of every taste. May my heart feed on Thee, on whom the Angels desire to look, and may my inmost soul be filled with the delightfulness of Thy taste. May my soul thirst for Thee, the well-spring of wisdom and knowledge, of life and light. May she seek Thee, the torrent of pleasure, the rich table of God's house. May she tend to Thee, find Thee,

meditate on Thee, speak of Thee, and do every work to the praise and glory of Thy name, with humility and prudence, love and pleasure, ease and affection, persevering to the end. And be Thou alone my hope, my salvation, confidence, riches, and joy, my rest and peace, my food, my refuge, my portion, my possession, my unfailing treasure, where my heart shall be ever firmly fixed. Amen.—*S. Bonaventura.*

96. SUPPLICATIONS.—O God, Father of our Lord Jesus Christ, who hearest all that rightly call upon Thee, and knowest the petitions of them that are silent, we give Thee thanks, for that Thou hast admitted us to these Thy holy mysteries for the increase of our piety, and the remission of our sins. And since Thou hast separated us from the wicked, to be Thy own peculiar people, strengthen us in the truth by Thy Holy Spirit. Reveal to us what we know not, and confirm us in the things we know. Hallow Thy priests, make kings to be peaceful, and magistrates just. Give healthy seasons, and plentiful harvests. Calm the turbulent, convert the erring, give perseverance to the good, establish the wavering, give fidelity to the married, and pure chastity to virgins. Gather us all into the kingdom of heaven in Christ our Lord, to whom be glory for ever and ever. Amen.

97. To the B. V. MARY.—Virgin Mother of my God, by the love with which thy Son, dying on the cross, commended thee to His beloved disciple, and His disciple in turn to thee, I

beseech thee to receive me to thy care and guardianship. Be with me in all the dangers and distresses of my whole life, and especially defend me at the hour of my death. Amen.

98. Abide with me, blessed Jesus, and be my continual safeguard, both of body and soul. Discover to me the ambushes of the wily foe, and put the enemy to flight by the display of Thy power, that by Thy protection within and without, I may securely arrive at the heavenly kingdom. Amen.

SATURDAY.—
BEFORE COMMUNION.

99. ADORATION.—O God, three in persons, one in substance, and Thou Lord Jesus Christ, true God and Man, I adore Thee with all my heart, and confess Thee as my Creator and last end. And as my adoration is so trivial, I offer also those excellent adorations paid Thee by Thy human nature, by the Blessed Virgin Mary, the whole court of heaven, and the holy Catholic Church Thy bride.—*St. Francis of Sales.*

100. LOVE.—Moreover, I love Thee, with all my heart, and mind, and strength; I love Thee above all things, and were it possible I would wish to love Thee with that most perfect love with which Thou lovest Thyself, and with which Thy human nature, Thy Virgin Mother, with the

whole Church in heaven and earth love Thee.—
S. Francis of Sales.

101. CONTRITION.—O my Lord, Thou art infinitely good, wise, just, and merciful. I grieve, then, for all my sins, mortal and venial; I detest them all, whether of thought, word, or deed, which from my first use of reason till this present hour I have committed. And as my sorrow is so imperfect, I offer instead the bitter tears of the prophet David, and those of S. Peter, and those shed by Mary Magdalen, and by all true penitents from the beginning of the world till now. Give me grace never to offend Thee again.—*Ditto.*

102. SATISFACTION.—As I can in no way satisfy, O Lord, for the debts I acknowledge to have incurred by my manifold offences, I offer to Thee the Passion and Death of Thy Only-begotten Son, asking pardon and grace. To it I add in satisfaction my whole life, my labours, sorrows and pains, which I humbly bear and will bear as a penance for my sins.—*Ditto.*

103. OBLATION.—With this surrender I offer and consecrate my whole self to Thy honour and glory, in union with that burning love and that most pure intention with which in the last supper Thou, my Jesus, didst give Thyself to us to be our Food, and with which Thou didst sacrifice Thyself as a bloody Victim on the altar of the cross. And to make up for my slender preparation and little devotion, I offer the lowliness, charity, and purity with which Thy most holy

Mother and other great saints have approached to this adorable Sacrament.—*S. Francis of Sales.*

104. To JESUS CHRIST.—Kindle, O Jesus, in my heart, which I offer to Thee as a holocaust, the fire of Thy love, and quench the flames of every earthly affection, that nothing may please me but only Thou. I wish my life and death to be an act of love.

Thou hast said, my Jesus, "Come to Me all ye that labour and are heavy laden, and I will refresh you." Thou waitest for me on the cross, with Thy arms wide stretched. I come, my Jesus, I come. Take me to the close embrace of Thy love, that I may ever be knit to Thee.

But I am commanded not to appear before Thee empty. What shall I give Thee, my Jesus? Receive what Thy own bounty has bestowed on me, all the powers of my soul, my memory, understanding, and will, which I consecrate to Thee. I wish to think only of Thee, to know nothing out of Thee, to love nothing beside Thee. Let Thy will, not mine, be done in all things. Amen.

105. To THE B. V. MARY.—Most chaste Virgin Mary, I ask thee, by that innocent purity by which thou didst make a pleasing mansion for the Son of God in thy virginal womb, to obtain by thy prayers that I may be cleansed from every stain.

Most lowly Virgin, I ask thee, by that profound humility which caused thee to be exalted above all the choirs of Saints and Angels, to obtain by thy prayers that I may be purged from all pride.

Most loving Virgin, I ask thee by that vehement love which knit thy holy soul inseparably to God, to obtain for me by thy prayers an abundance of ardent charity. Amen.

106. To THE SAINTS.—Angels, archangels, thrones, dominations, principalities, powers, virtues, cherubim, and seraphim, and all ye saints of God, especially N. N., whom we commemorate this day, help me by your prayers, that I may receive this Sacrament with a lively faith, a fervent love, and full devotion, and by a fruitful reception may be made one day worthy of your blessed company. Amen.

SATURDAY.—

AFTER COMMUNION.

107. ADORATION.—Hail, true Body, born of the Virgin Mary, which truly suffered and was sacrificed on the cross for man, whose pierced side flowed with water and blood. In death's dread trial be Thou our Food, O sweet Jesus! O tender Jesus! O Jesus, Son of Mary!

108. AFFECTIONS.—All wonder, O good Jesus, at Thy descending into the womb of Thy Mother Mary, though she was so pure, and full of every virtue and grace. Ought not, then, I much more to admire that Thou comest to lodge with me, so poor, so miserable a sinner? Thou, O Lord, the

Holy of Holies, hast vouchsafed to abide with me, who am a sink of sin. Hast Thou, then, been pleased so to honour me, so long an unclean vessel, as to make me Thy temple, Thy own tabernacle, and, as it were, a shrine for the relics of Thy Body and Blood, so far more holy than all the relics of the saints? May all Thy holy angels bless Thee for the favour Thou hast done to me. Give me grace to know how to possess my vessel ever in sanctification and honour, not in the passion of lust, as the Gentiles, who know not God.

Give me, dearest Jesus, to feel the blessed effects of Thy presence. I remember the benedictions which Thou hast heaped upon those who received Thee into their houses. Mary Thy Mother, when she received Thee into her womb, was filled with every gift of grace. Salvation came to the house of Zacheus when he took Thee within its walls. When after death Thou didst descend into limbo, it became by Thy presence a paradise. The house of Obededom was largely blessed by receiving the ark of the covenant. Bless, then, the house of my heart, into which Thou hast entered, and convert it into a paradise.

I remember, dearest Jesus, that in the holy Scripture it is said that the crowd sought to touch Thee, because virtue went out of Thee and healed all. Behold, I now have touched Thee, nay, I have even received Thee within me. Let virtue, then, go out of Thee to heal my soul, to cure it of every disease, and give it such strength that I may serve Thee in holiness and justice all the days of my life.

110. OBLATION AND PETITION.—I adore Thee, and I give Thee thanks, dearest Lord Jesus, who hast vouchsafed to admit me, a most vile sinner, to the rich banquet of Thy sacred table. Alas, how very unworthy is the reception I have given Thee. Pity me and pardon me. Receive this most excellent Sacrament as a full atonement for all my sins and negligences, as well as those of the whole world. I offer these holy mysteries for the honour of the most sweet Virgin Mary, Thy Mother, of all the Angels and Saints, and for the good of all the faithful, living and dead.

And I beseech Thee, eternal Father, let this Communion which I have received be beneficial to Thy whole Church. Take away from it all scandals and divisions. Let Thy mercy be upon the nations that know Thee not, and enlighten their hearts that they may learn to love Thee. Let the counsels of the wicked against Thy Church and Thy truth be defeated. To the Pope, our bishop, and all the clergy, give grace faithfully to fulfil their office. To kings and magistrates give wisdom rightly to govern and to distribute justice. Give true contrition to the dying. Give to my relations, friends, and benefactors every blessing, and to my enemies true charity. Give to the souls of the faithful in purgatory a merciful relief, and the enjoyment of beatitude.

111. FOR SINNERS.—O God, eternal Creator of all things, remember that the souls of sinners

were made by Thee, and that they are fashioned after Thy own image. Behold, O Lord, to Thy disgrace hell is filled with these. Remember that Jesus Thy Son died a most cruel death for their salvation. Do not permit them, then, any longer to persevere in their iniquities, and despise Thy Son, the Saviour of all; but, being appeased by the prayers of Thy Saints, and of Thy Church, the bride of Thy Son, be mindful of Thy mercy, and forgetting their disobedience and transgression, make them at length to be converted with their whole heart to Him whom Thou hast sent, our Lord Jesus Christ, by whom we are saved and redeemed, to whom be glory for ever and ever. 'Amen.—*S. Francis Xavier.*

112. To the B. V. Mary.—O blessed Mary, who can rightly sing thy praises, who by thy consent didst save the lost world? What blessings should not our frail human race give to thee, since by thee only has it found the entrance to life. Receive, then, these thanksgivings which are not equal to thy deserts, and receiving our vows, excuse our sins by thy prayers. By thee let that be pardoned which we have incurred; by thee let us obtain what with faithful mind we ask. Receive what we offer, give what we ask, excuse what we fear. Thou art the hope of sinners: through thee we look for our reward. Holy Mary, succour the miserable, help the fainthearted, comfort the weeping, pray for the people, mediate for the clergy, intercede for the

devout female sex, let all feel thy assistance who celebrate thy commemoration.

113. THE SAINTS.—O all ye Saints, look on me, and speak good things for me to the King of kings, who has fed me with His most precious Body and Blood. Offer to Him your merits to supply my shortcomings. Give thanks to Him for me, and ask Him not to withdraw His presence from me till He leave a double blessing behind Him.

114. CONCLUSION.—Let Thy grace help us, O Lord of hosts, that with all purity and devotion we may fulfil what we have this day promised Thee. And if we cannot live in such innocency of life as we ought, at least grant us worthily to lament the evils of which we are guilty, that in a spirit of humility, and purpose of good will, we may serve Thee all our days. Amen.

Indulgenced Prayers.

I.

I beseech of Thee, O most sweet Lord Jesus Christ, that Thy Passion may be to me strength to fortify, protect, and defend me: that Thy Wounds may be to me meat and drink, to feed, inebriate, and delight me: that the sprinkling of Thy Blood may wash away all my sins, and that Thy Death may be to me everlasting glory. In these may I take my repast, my joy, health, and sweetness of my heart. Who livest and reignest, world without end. Amen.

[Three years Indulgence for *priests* after **Mass**.]

II.

O Sacrament most holy! O Sacrament divine,
All praise and all thanksgiving be every moment Thine.

[100 days' Indulgence when said at the Elevation.]

III.

Look down, O Lord, from Thy sanctuary, and from heaven, Thy high dwelling place, and behold this sacred Host, which our great High Priest, Thy holy Child Jesus our Lord, offers to Thee for the sins of His brethren, and let Thy wrath for the multitude of our transgressions be appeased. Behold the Blood of our Brother Jesus cries to Thee from the cross. Graciously hear, O Lord! be merciful, O Lord! hearken and do; delay not, for Thy own sake, O my God, for Thy Name is called upon this city, and upon Thy people, but deal with us after Thy great mercy. Amen.

[One hundred days' Indulgence whenever said before the B. Sacrament. On the first Thursday in the month a Plenary Indulgence, when said after Communion.]

IV.

Blessed be God.
Blessed be His Holy Name.
Blessed be Jesus Christ, true God and true Man.
Blessed be the Name of Jesus.
Blessed be Jesus in the most holy Sacrament of the Altar.
Blessed be the great Mother of God, Mary most holy.
Blessed be her holy and Immaculate Conception.
Blessed be the name of Mary, Virgin and Mother.
Blessed be God in His Angels and in His Saints.

[One years' Indulgence each time said, and plenary once a month after Communion, when said daily.]

V.

My Jesus, mercy. [100 days each time.]

VI.

Sweet Heart of Mary, be my salvation.

[300 days each time: plenary once a month.]

VII.

Look down upon me, good and gentle Jesus, while before Thy Face I humbly kneel, and with burning soul, pray and beseech Thee to fix deep in my heart lively sentiments of faith, hope, and charity, true contrition for my sins, and firm purpose of amendment, while I contemplate, with great love and tender pity, Thy Five Wounds, pondering over them within me, whilst I call to mind the words, which David Thy prophet said of Thee, my Jesus: *They pierced My Hands and My Feet; they numbered all My bones.*

[A Plenary Indulgence after Communion.]

Visiting the B. Sacrament.

✠

At a Visit the following Prayers will be found suitable.

Invocation of the Holy Ghost, 87.
Adoration, 33, 55, 99, 108.
Humility, 6, 34.
Contrition, 2, 17, 65, 84, 101, 102.
Faith, Hope, and Charity, 3, 18, 36, 65, 85.
The Passion, 91, 105.
Affections, 8, 15, 23, 42, 43, 74, 75, 78, 90, 95, 109.
Oblation, 10, 11, 12, 30, 36, 57, 77, 95.
Supplications, 31, 58, 96.
Conversion of Sinners, 112.
Reparation, 94,
Thanksgiving, 61.]
To B. V. M., 13, 26, 47, 59, 71, 88, 97, 106, 113.
To the Saints, 14, 27, 41, 60, 81, 89, 114.

Richardson and Son, Printers, Derby.

www.ingramcontent.com/pod-product-compliance
Lightning Source LLC
Chambersburg PA
CBHW020244090426
42735CB00010B/1825